The First Christmas

Peggy K. Comer   Illustrations by Rebekah Lauzier

2019 White Bird 1st Edition

Copyright © 2019 by Peggy R. Comer
Illustrations by Rebekah Lauzier

Published in the United States by
White Bird Publication, LLC, Texas
www.whitebirdpublications.com

ISBN 978-1-63363-433-6
eBook ISBN 978-1-63363-434-3
Library of Congress Control Number 2019948574

I dedicate this book to children, young and old, everywhere, who have heard the story from God's Word about the birth of Jesus Christ in the little town of Bethlehem. This truly was the "First Christmas" as the GREATEST GIFT of all times was ushered in as a tiny baby in a manger. How glorious that lowly shepherds were the first to hear and proclaim the good news! Many of you have dressed up as shepherds or angels in church pageants over the years, and I hope the illustrations help you recall those times with fondness.

Rebekah—Thank you for your patience as we worked on the illustrations together. It was difficult at times for me to communicate to you exactly what I was seeing in my mind for each page, but how awesome it was to finally exclaim, "Yes! This is it! Love it!" You are amazing, and I was blessed to have you work alongside me in the production of this book

LMBC Bible Study Ladies—I cannot thank you enough for the encouragement you give me each week, and for the prayers lifted up on my behalf as we hunger to learn more as we study God's Word together. Many of you were praying specifically for this book. As Paul said in Philippians 1:3, "I thank my God upon every remembrance of you…"

Grace, Andrew, Austin, Nathan and Addison—I am so blessed and thankful for my grandchildren. You keep me "young at heart!" Addison, this book is especially for you, because I was blessed to see your love of reading flourish as we memorized Cubby and Sparks (AWANA) Bible verses together. You are all loved more than words could ever express.

Most of all, I thank God for sending His Son, Jesus Christ, to be my Lord and Savior. May He be glorified in all my writings.

IN NEARBY FIELDS, SHEPHERDS WERE TENDING THEIR FLOCK OF SHEEP. THEY WERE MOST LIKELY SEATED AROUND A CAMPFIRE, DISCUSSING THE EVENTS OF THE DAY. A LITTLE BLACK AND WHITE LAMB HAD TO BE RESCUED FROM FALLING OFF THE CLIFF; THE LITTLE

TWIN LAMBS WANTED
TO BE HELD ALL DAY,
AND THE BIG OLD EWE
WAS CONSTANTLY STARTING
TROUBLE WITH SOME
OF THE YOUNGER EWES
AND RAMS. BUT OTHER
THAN THE USUAL THINGS
THAT GO ON IN THE DAILY
LIVES OF SHEPHERDS,
EVERYTHING WAS
PERFECTLY ORDINARY...

UNTIL SOMETHING QUITE SPECTACULAR AND OUT OF THE ORDINARY HAPPENED!

IT WAS THE NIGHT OF THE VERY FIRST CHRISTMAS, AND THE SHEEP WERE ALL BEDDED DOWN;

THE SHEPHERDS WERE RESTING AND TALKING, WHEN A BRIGHT LIGHT SHONE ALL AROUND!

THEN AN ANGEL APPEARED
OUT OF NOWHERE,
WITH A MESSAGE STRAIGHT
FROM ABOVE.

HE SAID, "NO NEED TO BE FRIGHTENED, I COME WITH A MESSAGE OF LOVE!

I BRING GOOD NEWS FOR ALL PEOPLE... A PROMISE FULFILLED WITH MUCH JOY!

UNTO YOU IS BORN IN THE CITY OF DAVID, THE SAVIOR, JESUS CHRIST, A SWEET PRECIOUS BOY!

*TO PROVE THIS NEWS IS
FROM HEAVEN,
THERE IS A SIGN THAT TO
YOU MAY SEEM LOWLY;*

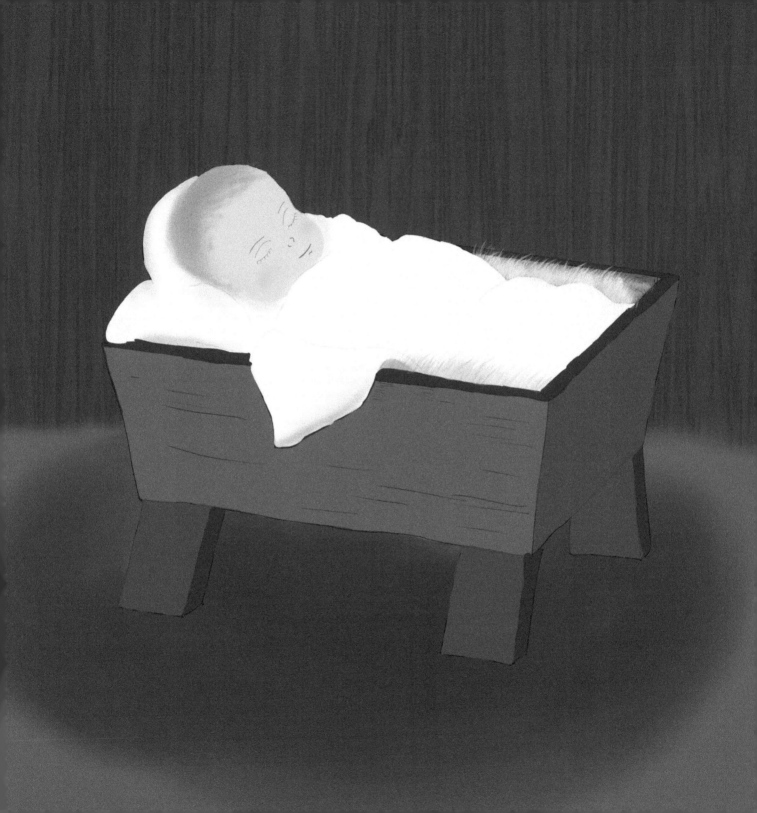

YOU WILL FIND THE BABE WRAPPED IN SWADDLING CLOTHES IN A MANGER—ALTHOUGH HE IS MOST HOLY!

AND SUDDENLY THERE WAS
WITH THE ANGEL,
A MULTITUDE OF THE
HEAVENLY HOST WHO
BEGAN,

PRAISING AND SINGING GLORY TO GOD IN THE HIGHEST, PEACE ON EARTH AND GOOD WILL TOWARD MEN!"

THEN THE ANGELS WENT BACK TO HEAVEN, AND THE SHEPHERDS EXCLAIMED, "THAT WAS QUITE A FRIGHT!

LET'S GO TO BETHLEHEM TO SEE FOR OURSELVES, WHAT'S BEEN PROCLAIMED TO US THIS NIGHT."

WITH HASTE THEY MADE
THEIR WAY TOWARD THE
TOWN,
AND I IMAGINE THEY MADE
QUITE A SIGHT,

CARRYING BABY LAMBS ON THEIR SHOULDERS; WAS THERE EVER A NIGHT SO BRIGHT?

COULD THIS BE THE PLACE?
A STABLE LIKE THIS ONE?
THE ANIMALS WERE ALL STANDING AT BAY.

AND JUST AS THE ANGEL
HAD TOLD THEM...
A BABY WAS ASLEEP ON THE
HAY!

HOW EXCITING TO BE THE FIRST TO HEAR SUCH NEWS, REJOICING, THEY TOLD EVERYONE THEY MET!

THIS WAS CERTAINLY THE NEWS OF THE AGES; IT WAS A NIGHT THEY WOULD NEVER FORGET!

CPSIA information can be obtained
at www.ICGtesting.com
Printed in the USA
LVHW071736041119
636280LV00020B/536/P